It Happened To Me…

Written by Kristin Schanks,
Weston, FL.

KRISTIN SCHANKS,
WESTON, FL.

It Happened To Me...

ISBN 978-1-234-56789-1

"Everything is going to be alright..."

Table of Contents

I dedicate this story to

my loving mother.

Prologue

It was a dark stormy night in mid-June, where one could hear the roaring
of the treacherous thunder
and see those on going flashes of lightning that were a million times brighter than any camera flash and it'd seemed to vanish in a split second; one could take in
the gross, muddy humid rain water streaming down
the sidewalk clustered with
small dirt particles or grass, but they ran into a

small halt as they approached the red all-star
converse shoe of a young boy only eleven years of age by the name of Timothy Cornelius Stewart.

He was a scrawny little boy, with dark silky smooth coffee colored hair,
and deep intricate blue eyes; he had pale skin that
was icy cold to the touch, his clothes were all filthy and dirty like he was outside all day, he seemed
to be walking on his own taking in some of the fresh

rain water as he kept his tongue sticking out. He seemed care free in despite of the vicious and quite rough storm that was occurring – although nobody really knew what was going on in Timothy's life. Timothy hadn't even started his teen years yet, but already his life was a battle to uphold, he faced many despicable things no other children of his age would normally see happen.

Chapter 1

At the age of five Timothy's real father, Ethan Hollow, kicked out his mother and him from their home. It was September 24th on a luminous, upbeat Sunday afternoon when all of the sudden Timothy's father’s inner wrath and actualities came out in an aggressive manner, it turned out he found another woman much younger in her early twenties; she was thin as a twig and fragile as if she

was some type of fine China, she was at a decent height for being a girl, she had beach blond curly hair
with baby blue eyes, and she had a surfers type of tan; she had also seemed to keep herself in shape. On the contrary to his real mother, Olivia, who was in
her early thirties with dull,
lifeless brunette hair, a fair, unsoiled skin tone, she had sparkling chocolate colored eyes, she
smelled like soothing vanilla and refreshing strawberries; also, she had

a typical body for someone her age.

Ethan decided to proclaim that he cheated on Olivia when he got fed up hearing Timothy's whining and crying over a *Spongebob* ice-cream popsicle when Timothy heard the sticker covered brick shaped ice-cream truck drive by with its merry jingle playing aloud.

While Olivia was fixing up some brunch, but out of her exhaustion she left the meat loaf she was making in the oven for a bit too long. As a result, causing the smoke alarm to go off like a child screaming for help, while the house was being consumed in the aroma of burning fumes, however it was nothing too serious, even though the house seemed to be a jumble at the moment. All this raucous seemed to really agitate Ethan and it caused him to get a loose wire in his brain, and for the first time ever; he just completely lost it.

Ethan violently argued with Olivia; he yelled out the truth in a frightening manner, what
he honestly thought of her,
how hideous and aged she had become to him, how
she no longer satisfied him,
all she would do is nag about not getting any help
around the house, he cursed at her ruthlessly while shaking his scrunched fist in front of her face, he insulted her

repeatedly in front of Timothy who began to turn ruby red due to all the fuming and tension Ethan was lashing out at her. He told her he had been cheating on her with his assistant at work and that's why he would come home late every night and most importantly he told her; he no longer loved her – she was meaningless to him.

Olivia just broke down after hearing

all of that, she gradually fell to the ground; tears filled her now puffy red eyes, her hands trembled uncontrollably, her russet hair became a untamed mess, one could hear her sobbing while her quivering hands tried to cover her eyes throughout this chaos, she just kept repeating in a cheerless and terrified manner, "Why? Why me? I'm sorry Ethan, just please, please don't leave me..." Ethan replied in an impatient, yet irritated manner, "Just go,

and leave my sight,
NOW!"
But, Olivia kept saying
no,
she didn't want to go,
they
could work things out;
that
caused Ethan to become
even more infuriated
than
ever, so he decided to
hastily and intolerantly
walk up to Olivia with
one
wicked thought in his
mind. He raised his hand
back then smacked her
across the face with his
giant, ragged hand; it
slashed a bit of her rosy
pink bottom lip causing
her to bleed a bit, she

didn't know what to do or what to think; she was petrified. Ethan grabbed some of her things, and threw it at her, then shouted, "Scram already, you worthless piece of garbage!"

Olivia scurried out the door while clasping onto Timothy's little hand.

In the end, Timothy and Olivia never spoke nor saw Ethan again.

Chapter 2

When Timothy turned eight years old Olivia had decided to

remarry with a man by the
name of Cameron Stewart.
He was in his late thirties;
he was quite tall, he had short, dark chaotic brown
hair, exotic jade piercing eyes, pale skin, and his voice was profound; it seemed overbearing to many. He was sincere, but
Timothy didn't want to accept the fact that was now his new father.

Timothy began to rebel a little after his mother got married; he would leave a mess around wherever he went, such as leaving his *Marvel* action figure toys out causing James to accidently step on it and get hurt by it. Or, he would yell back at Olivia whenever she didn't get what Timothy wanted.

Also, he would go outside telling his mother he would play for twenty minutes, but he wouldn't come back inside the house for hours on purpose just to make her worry.

But, Timothy stopped doing things like that for a while, because on December 25th while they were sitting down by
the warm crackling open fire, sharing silly Christmas stories, and opening presents the doctor called the house telling them the result of Olivia's tests; since she hadn't been feeling well for
a few months now. The doctor said she was diagnosed with breast cancer.

Chapter 3

Timothy was now ten years of age, he couldn't imagine life without his beautiful mother, she was
the only thing he ever had
that never left; that always
stood by his side and in fact cared about him. Timothy didn't know what
to do anymore, he was unsure of everything; he'd have random moments of frustration where he would let all of inner anger out by punching things – where he would just break down and cry.

One day Olivia and Timothy were at the dock by the lake, she told him, "Everything will be fine Timothy, please don't cry; I've been going to chemo-therapy and it will help me get better. The doctors know what they're doing. I'll be okay-" Timothy promptly interrupted by saying, "Yeah, but what if it doesn't work? What if I lose you and you die? What if you'll never be here for me to see or talk to again? What if I never get the chance to ever hug you again when I'm feeling

down mommy? What if I fall down and cut myself and you're not there to kiss
it and make it feel all better? What if you never see me grow-up? I don't want to say good-bye…I just can't."

Olivia's eyes glistened as she began to tear up; her voice trembled
a bit in a low calming tone
as she simply replied, "Timothy, if I do die, you will *never* be alone. You may not see me nor hear me, but I will always be there with you. I promise

you that. I will protect you
through whatever and make sure you're okay. But, if you ever need to talk to me, then at night I'll
visit you in your dreams, I'll be there to talk to you.
Whenever you hear the birds chirping, it'll be me singing to you, when it rains, I'll be the rainbow afterwards making sure that you smile, when the seasons change it's me bringing you to a better time in your life, and when
it's winter and you begin to
feel a bit chilly, I'll be the

warmth from the fireplace place, because I'm giving you a hug. So, don't mope my handsome boy, you are more astonishing and strong than you'll ever know. Keep smiling that magnificent smile that God has blessed you with…I love you Timothy."

Timothy didn't speak another word, instead he wrapped his little arms around his mother hugging her tightly and never wanting to let go; as Olivia would gently stroke her strained hand through his silky-smooth brown hair with tears slowly streamed down her face; she couldn't help but feeling a bit torn apart by all of this.

Timothy would constantly be in his room, praying that his mother's cancer would just go away and that their life could return to normal. Timothy tried to change for the better, so his mother could be pleased and maybe that would make her cancer go away.

During this time, Cameron and Timothy had begun to get along a little better.

Chapter 4

However, on November 19th at Richmond Hospital at 2:34
p.m. Olivia Stewart passed
away. Timothy had gotten
himself all fixed up and everything that day; he brushed his hair with gel,

he wore a brand-new white *American Eagle* collar shirt, he brushed his teeth about seven times with *Aqua Fresh* tooth-paste, and he put on a fancy cologne made by *Hugo Boss*.

Timothy felt blissful inside; he couldn't stop smiling all that morning. It was his eleventh birthday and his mother said she had a surprise for him the day before.

But, when he got to

the hospital at 3:00 p.m. they told him Olivia had died. Timothy felt like all the air was knocked right
out of him, like his heart has been shredded into a million pieces then beaten
with a hammer, he felt motionless at first then ran
to her hospital room which
was *A245*. Everything around him seemed nonexistent,
one could hear
him running across the cerulean plastic hospital tiles as he was gasping for

air, then he slammed open
the old creaking wooden door, and saw that her bed
was neatly fixed up; the blankets were folded, there
were new sheets, the nightstand
was empty – it
almost seemed like she never existed.

Then a nurse walked in and Timothy shouted with mixed emotions, “Why
didn’t you tell me sooner?! I wasn’t there to tell her
good-bye! She was all by

herself! I wanted to give my
mommy a hug and a kiss!
But, now she's gone! It's my birthday; I didn't want
her to leave! Why did she have to go? Why? Oh, why?!" He began to weep; he tried wiping away his tears with his black jacket
sleeve. The nurse didn't know what to say, she simply shed a tear that streamed down the side of
her auburn face, and then
said in a low distraught voice, "She left this for you..." The nurse handed

him a tiny velvet red box.

Timothy slowly lifted up his thin petite arm to reach the box; his hand was
trembling a bit from all the
grief and sorrow he was feeling at the moment.

When he finally held the
box and he gently opened
it; inside was a shiny, gold
elegant pocket-watch and
when he clicked it open there was a photo of him and his mother together when he was a baby. When

he closed the watch on the
cover of it a few measly word were inscribed on it that read, *"I will always love you Timothy,"* then after that it showed a little
heart next to the words, "Mommy."

Timothy sobbed nonstop
after that; he felt as if life as he knew it stopped,
as if he were in some alternate universe. He couldn't accept the fact that his mother was gone;
that his mother was now died. He couldn't feel

anything, but wretchedness and anguish.
He wanted to go to his mommy and hug her, but
he knew he couldn't do that anymore...

For the next few weeks Timothy would walk
around in a forest that surrounded him; he felt bewildered. He would walk
along an old grimy dock that was at the end of the
forest, he felt at peace there; looking along the shore as he saw the trifling

serene waves in the lake brush against a stream of
rocks. He would go there whenever he wanted to think; he thought about life, his mother, and what
was the purpose of his mother's death.

Everyone says, "Everything happens for a reason," well Timothy thought what could have possibly been that reason? His mother never hurt
anyone, she never lied nor cheated, she never swore
or cursed, and now that Timothy looked back at

it...she lived a miserable life. His mother was kicked
out of her home in Minnesota at the age of sixteen and expected to make it all on her own; she
never got to finish high school, so she ended up with some average cheap minimum wage pay at some office. Her first husband cheated on her with his assistant and he had the nerve to brutally abuse her, and she ended
up dying from breast cancer. Timothy began to yell and cry as he smashed his hands against the

rocks and filthy floor filled with twigs, pebbles, and sticks; he in fact missed her and wished his mother had a better life.

Whenever Timothy got home Cameron seemed to always ask him if he wanted to go out for ice-cream or if he wanted a new video game. But, Timothy just nodded, “no,” then he went to bed.

For, the next three months Timothy was like that.

Chapter 5

When he went to school he just got in trouble with some of the other kids, sometimes he would reply harshly and erratically to some of the boys letting out his fury at them. He skipped school at times; he just didn't want to do anything anymore and his grades were going down. Also, some of the boys would pick and tease Timothy for not having a mother; they would tell him "What are you going to do about it? Run home to your mommy? Oh, wait you can't," then they would chuckle maliciously. That soon got on Timothy's nerves; he told them one day they would regret saying things like that to him.

On one sundrenched Tuesday afternoon in the month of March, Timothy was walking along a dusty sidewalk cluttered with fresh

cut grass while dribbling his old, worn-out basketball when it suddenly hit the tip of his
black and white leather Nike shoe and began to roll
away. It landed at the footsteps of the Seventh Day Adventist Church; the
priest at the church stepped out and picked up
the basketball and handed
it to Timothy. Timothy jerked the ball away quickly without saying, “thank you” or even a smile.

The priest then said, "You're welcome to come in," then he grinned. Timothy unkindly replied by saying, "No, I don't need
to be wasting my time at place like that." The priest
then said, "Well young man, some place like that
will always be here for you
if you ever need someone to talk to or a place to think." Timothy answered
back saying, "Yeah yeah, well I'm gonna go."

Later that day

Timothy went to Drew's house; Drew was the leader of the boys that bullied him at school. Timothy was overflowing with rage and fury; he scrunched a rigid brick with a flimsy note tied around to it in one hand while the other held a fresh can of crimson spray paint. Timothy's pulse sped up with each step he took, his hands quivered as anxiety was flowing throughout him and he

only had one clear thought
in his mind – revenge. He went up to the side of Drew's modern stylish azure colored house then he began to spray crude offensive words on the walls of Drew's home expressing his hatred towards him; the inner wrath he had truthfully felt
then he threw the burgundy brick straight through Drew's window causing it to savagely shatter.

Inside the home one could overhear the screeching of an adolescent

calling out to his parents as they frantically race up
the stairs; Timothy soon fled the scene as fast as his
legs could take him; he was heading towards the dump so he could throw away the spray paint.

Chapter 6

The next day at school Drew showed up with a green fiber cast and
when he saw Timothy he gave him a death glare, as
almost as if he is saying, "I'm going to get you for

this."

After school as Timothy was walking home, he could sense something was wrong, when he decided to glance back and he could see Drew and his crew were following him. Timothy began to scamper away; his heart was beating faster than a drum solo at a concert, he was plagued with fright, he began to get colorless when he realized how appalling it was of him to do what he did the day

before, he just wanted to fade away at the moment,
he could feel his throat beginning to ache, he began to get dehydrated, he was almost home when
they suddenly caught him.
He kept blaring in agony, "Let me go! Let me go! Somebody help me!" In hopes that somebody would hear his cry, but Drew then wrapped duct tape over his mouth to keep him quite while they
dragged him deep into the
woods.

Then Drew said wildly, "I know it was you, I saw the note on the brick saying, '*I told you, you would regret it,*' well now it's time for some pay back!" Then Drew cracked his fists as the boys soon crowded around Timothy forming a circle; making him feel powerless and inferior to them.

They began to cruelly cuff him in the face, kicking him brutally in his tender little stomach, while calling him a loser, stupid, ugly, a waste of life, they said his mother should've died earlier, so someone like him would've never been born, and other inhuman things they cold-bloodedly told him. One could hear Timothy's earsplitting cries through the duct tape, it was a cry begging them to stop, one see his face turning bloody red almost purple, he felt an intense amount of pain while he curled up into a ball with his arms juddering fiercely, he was losing his breath, his eyes puffed up as he sobbed. After fifteen to twenty minutes of torture for Timothy one of the boys said, “Let’s go, I think we got him enough, plus my mom might start worry…” Drew replied saying, “Alright,” then lashed out at Timothy about three more times then left.

Timothy bawled; he peeled off the duct tape hurriedly, then he began to gasp for air, he just stayed laying there at the moment, screaming at the top of his lungs, he just wanted to die at that moment.

Unexpectedly, a brush of wind struck him; something told him to go back to the priest that he saw the day before. So, Timothy picked himself up, patted the dirt off of himself and decided to slowly walk back through his pain to the Seventh Day Adventist Church to see the priest.

When he arrived the

priest's face filled with fright as he saw the condition Timothy was in;
they discussed what Timothy had done. The priest said, "Don't worry my boy, God will help you
through this, God knows what he is doing. Life has
many ups and downs, but
considering the fact that you've faced many downs so earlier in your life, I'm sure later on more positive
things will occur for you You seem like a brilliant young boy, and don't let

that go to waste – one
day
you'll do something
astonishing I just know
it.
So, continue with school
and improve your work
habits, you just may
discover something
about
yourself you didn't know
before. Your mother is
still
watching you; she wants
to
see you do the right
things.
Timothy, God does love
you, he loves everyone,
and
the moment you ask for
forgiveness, God will
forgive you for your sins,

he holds no grudges. I promise you, the moment you start believing, hoping, and having faith in God, everything will be alright. Also, don't listen to those boys from school, all they want to do is bring you down, don't let them do that to you. You will do great things one day; just make a change for the better today."

Timothy cried tears of relief, he felt like he made the right choice by coming to here, then he

hugged the priest and said,
"Thank you."

The next day Timothy decided to go to his mother's grave to leave her some of her favorite flowers by her tombstone, and tell her, he's doing alright and he knows she's looking after him.

Chapter 7

For the next few years or so Timothy got along with Cameron better and they soon became best friends, he visited the Seventh Day Adventist Church every day, his education levels improved and he started getting honor rolls, awards, and got into gifted classes. Timothy finally knew what he wanted to do with his life, one day he wanted to open up his own orphanage for the children who are facing difficult times in their life without any parents. He wants to make those children feel

loved, cared for, he wants
them to have hope for a brighter future; he wants those children to know they are a miracle from God, a gift from above, not
a regret like how he felt for
a while.

Timothy would think about his mother every now and then. He missed and still loved her. But, he
knew she was still with him in spirit.

When Timothy began his senior year at Rye High
School, he was expecting

another typical year, yet he was eager as well, because he was one year closer to starting his college year at Harvard University to earn his business degree; he got accepted into Harvard's business school over the summer. In the month of November, he decided to switch one of his classes with AP Psychology and that's the day he met Amy Schwartz; she seemed like a queen, high and regal with big baby blue shimmering eyes deep as the Pacific ocean, she had flawless fair skin, an ideal figure, that every girl desires to have in their dreams. She also appeared to be light as a feather, and she had long dark wavy hair that cascaded like a waterfall down her back, reaching almost to her waist. Timothy instantly felt a rush of emotions – he knew he had fallen in love with her.

After class that day Timothy chased after her to

the courtyard of their school, he asked her if she could help him study for an exam; soon afterwards they became best

friends.

He loved how she could walk into a room and her flamboyantly wild, yet joyful spirit could light up a room, or how whenever she giggled he felt like he heard the sweet laugher of an angel, how her hugs could instantly cheer him up, everything about Amy was exquisite to Timothy. He was madly in love with Amy; no amount of Shakespeare or any other love story novelist could compare with what he had felt for her.

Amy was the inspiration in his life, he would visit her every day and Timothy always brought his Canon 7D camera with him to school; so Amy and him could take pictures together.

Timothy felt like

Amy was the only person who in all truthfulness understood him. She accepted his faults in his past, she knew what he loved, what he disliked, and what his passion in life
was; Timothy could trust telling Amy anything in confidence – she owned

his heart.

On February 14th, Timothy finally decided to
ask her to be his girlfriend.
He told her, “You’re the most remarkable, benevolent, and brilliantly
radiant person I’ve ever

known. Your smile makes me feel like the world is saying, *'everything is going to be alright'*, your voice is the melody to my heart, your eyes are so luminously pure, just like your spirit, my one wish that only you could make come true is…will you be my girlfriend?" He held his arms open wide, while holding a pink rose in his right hand with a small burgundy Hershey chocolate gift box in the other; he began to blush.

Amy's eyes gleamed as they filled with tears of
delight. She immediately shouted, "Yes!" She told him she wanted him to ask
her that for a long time and she wrapped her arms
tightly around him. Timothy had the biggest smile on his face, he felt like the luckiest man on earth; most people search
for love their whole life, but
he was fortunate enough to find it at a young age.

They were the most superb couple that one could ever see, Timothy always gave Amy a surprise hug from behind, he would call her beautiful every day; in the morning, afternoon, and night, so she would never forget how dazzling she was. Also, Amy was a stunning artist; she loved to sketch Timothy in her free time. She would tell him he was her muse; Timothy would cherish all of her art works.

They would play in

the snow or take walks on the beach, he would sometimes setup a gazebo that he has in the back yard with white Christmas lights to illuminate the scene, while scattering pink carnation petals across the ground and play some cheesy 1950's romantic music; he would take Amy there and they would dance all night long forgetting any retched problems they had.

Whenever they were

together the world felt motionless, like time stood
completely still for them, and like their love would stop any danger or destruction from coming

to them.

Timothy enjoyed surprising her with daisy's,
he would give her random
light kisses on her forehead or her tender cheek as she began to blush. Timothy only felt pleased when he saw Amy
satisfied; her happiness meant the world to him.

Sometimes they would
lay
on a blanket out in a
field
and watch the stars at
night, seeing how they
glistened, with their
eccentric delicacy in
their
harmonious
surroundings;
this made Timothy think.
Timothy would tell her
he
would never hurt her, he
wouldn't be like his
father, Ethan, he
wouldn't dare
abandon her. Timothy
would sometimes read
her
a succinct poem that he

wrote about his feelings
for her, and then he
would
normally whisper *I love
you*
to her when he was
done.
She was his world – his
life and they would
spend
every waking moment
together; they were
inseparable.

People would tell
Timothy he couldn't say
he's in love; he's just a
kid.
But Timothy would tell
them, "Then call me
crazy,
because my girl is one
beauty I'll never let go of,

she taught me what true love is, what it's like to trust and care for something, she is my princess, my lucky charm,
my fairytale come to life, so
go ahead and think what you want to think, but I know what I feel for her."

Timothy adored how her hair shined in the beaming sunlight, how she
always smelled like fresh cherry blossoms, how her eyes could still shimmer
even on the darkest of nights, how whenever they

held hands he got butterflies in his stomach,
he loved how she would flutter her eyelashes, or how she never seemed to try, but she always did amaze him, he loved her spontaneous, kind-hearted
spirit, and when their lips
touched softly, lovingly, they breathed in their souls and their love into each other in every kiss. Their kisses were firm, yet tender – sweltering but
refreshing. It would only be for a split second, but it

seemed to last a lifetime. In each kiss, it made his love her grow even more than the last.

Amy was ravishing without a doubt, plus she
also wanted to start her own orphanage someday too. Timothy knew who he
wanted to marry one day,
he had his heart set on Amy. They would talk about getting married all the time, in the spring where one could view all the cheery flowers blossoming with enthusiasm as they were being reborn, in a lush farm type of field they

would have their
reception
and in the Seventh Day
Adventist Church they'd
recite their vows with a
few
guests and the priest
Timothy met as a child
being there on their
glorious day.

Timothy and Amy
would lie on the grass;
seemingly twirling their
fingers around together
as
she rested her head
tenderly on his chest
being
able to hear the soft
beating of his calm
heart, looking up at the

clouds and thinking
about
their life together
someday;
living in a big old white
house, with vibrant
daisy's
filling the front yard,
having five bedrooms,
and a fancy
white dining room, and
having a baby girl
someday
named Emma. They
pinky
promised each other they
would grow old together
and stick together no
matter what, they would
work-out any situation
or
problem they would run
into; they would stay

together forever with
never ending
love.

Chapter 8

Now Timothy was twenty-five years old and he was at the most thriving
time of his life; he graduated from Harvard. He was looked up to by a countless number of people
they felt moved by his life story when they read a column about it in *Times* magazine. Timothy still thought of his mother every once in a while, but

he knew he had to live his
life with an optimistic attitude for Amy – he wanted to be the finest man he could be, since he
would be her future husband in May. Not to mention, that last Christmas he opened up his fifth orphanage that was called, "*Olivia's Home.*"
He felt proud that he accomplished something miraculous in his life far, he felt like God had given him a second chance
to live his life right, he knew his mother was his guardian angel; she was

still with him in spirit. He felt eternally grateful to God everyday of his life he was given, every second of the day, he couldn't have done any of these things without his aid. God knew what he was doing – what Timothy's true fate was in life.

On May 25th, Timothy saw the birds flying home and the flowers budding. He smelled the fresh air, not full of cold or frost, but

of warmth and glee. Timothy sensed the butterflies, swarming around him, landing on him for good fortune. The sounds of springtime brightened up Timothy's day, he could hear the children running to school
or playing in the park as he took a quick sip of ice cold lemonade before he had to get ready for his wedding day.

Later on when Timothy finally saw Amy take her first steps down the red velvet carpet aisle filled with white rose petals, he could hear the classical wedding music

play soothingly on the grand piano, he felt a bit weak as the nerves hit him,
he cried a bit, yet he felt merry, but he wanted his mother to be there, to be sitting in the stands, to see
him on his big day, he sneakily pulled out the pocket-watch she had given him and held it firmly in his youthful hands to calm his

nerves.

But, he stared at Amy in awe as she gracefully moved down the
aisle in her cream colored

dress flowing freely like tranquil ocean waters, her
hair put up into a chic bun
with a glittery snow veil on
top, her lips were strawberry pink, she battered her eyes with ease, as she kept that contagious smile of hers. Timothy's heart raced faster than an Olympic gold medalist, he knew everything was going to be
alright from this moment on and their expedition as
husband and wife would soon begin.

Timothy had always thought that true love is something basically indescribable. But, his closest way as to defining it
was a person that knows the value and the imperfections in you, yet they still accept you wholeheartedly and unconditionally. Someone
who wants' to hold you in
their arms gently, beyond
security, prestige, triumph,
or wanting to play around
with you; just to say once

and for all, "*I love you*", and mean it from the top of their head to-the-depths of their heart. This is the type of love that casts out fright; that makes life worth living. True love takes a man and woman on this earth and lifts them above every influence or ache that could wound them. Timothy felt like he and Amy had something, strong and pure like that; he knew he was making the right choice.

When she finally stood in front of Timothy and they finished telling their I do's, he leaned in for
the kiss, he gently brushed
her cheek as they breathed
in synchronized formation,
they looked intensely into
each other's immense sapphire eyes, then their passionate lips met; Timothy never felt so alive
– so invigorating. It felt like
an endless enchantment.

Chapter 9

On December 12th, Timothy bought her an enormous old white country house; the same type of house they would constantly talk about – dream about. It was more
impressive then how Amy
ever imagined it. It was truly breathtaking; she cried tears of exuberance from its ravishing beauty.
She felt like they took another giant leap into their true-life journey together.

The years went by and now Timothy was in

his late twenties
energized
with how well his charity
benefit fundraisers had
been going, along with
his
grand feeling knowing
that their first child was
on the
way; Amy was already
three months into labor
and they were expecting
a
divine little girl by the
name of Emma. Amy was
overjoyed at the thought
of
being a mother; she
would
clean the house often to
keep herself busy to
sooth
some of her nerves

whenever she became overwhelmed.

On a bitter, dark Monday evening when Amy was mopping the floor with some of *Mr. O'Brandy Magic Floor Cleaner;* she kept her hair tied up into a messy bun, as she swayed the mop across her vintage mahogany wooden floor when the house phone began to ring, she bellowed to Timothy to answer it, but it seemed like Timothy

never heard her; because he never responded. Amy decided to go answer it as
she began walking across
the creaking floor boards beneath her she took her first step to go down the stairs. She missed the first
step at the top and tumbled down, banging and scraping herself on her
way down. Timothy ran to
her in fear as to what he might find, he goes up to her while dialing 911 on his cell phone. He held her in his arms; her mouth

was gushing blood, because she bashed her chin on one of the steps. Amy was bawling; her eyes became an extreme shade of red, and they puffed up as well, she was screaming from this immense amount of pain that was upon her, and she clenched her stomach firmly.

Timothy began to cry from all this panic and terror; he didn't want to see her in all this pain. He

rushed her to the
hospital
himself for hours and
hours they never told
him
how it was going; if she
would be ok. He waited
and waited, eventually
he
just feel asleep in a dull
maroon chair in the
lobby
and woke up the next
day
with a light tap on the
shoulder by one of the
doctors, he stood tall and
rigid, almost
emotionless;
he didn't want to look
directly into Timothy's
eyes.

Then he spoke in a monotone voice without any true sympathy as if he
says these things every day, he said, “Amy is fine,
she is resting. However, I’m
sorry to tell you, but your
baby didn’t make it due to
complications. Amy’s fall was just too dramatic for the baby to take. I’m sorry.” Then he tried to pat
Timothy on the shoulders,
but Timothy just told him
to leave him alone, he

didn't want the man's pity.

Timothy couldn't breathe anymore, he felt the world rushing around him while he was the only one staying in place falling deeper into misery, he looked at his white strained hands that were beginning to tremble violently, his voice vanished he couldn't speak not even the slightest of words. Then he remembered Amy, it gave

him the strength to get up and he rushed to her. He
slammed open her hospital
door at room A245; it was
his mothers old room. He showered her with kisses and then he cuddled her on the bland metallic hospital bed; their affectionate love for one another kept each other feeling a little better.

He kept reminding her how much he loved her
as she wept how regretful
and remorseful she was that they lost the baby,

because of her mistake.

For the next month or so, they both fell into a
profound state of depression. Neither of them
spoke much to one another
anymore, they smiled less
and cried more; the loss of
the baby began to tear them apart. Sometimes Amy would go into the room they made for their unborn baby girl and she would rock back and forth
on an old white creaking

rocking chair while holding a beige plush rabbit that was meant for Emma as she wept her eyes out.

Timothy would just go out for walks in the forest again like he did when he was a child; he felt the trees surrounding him once more as the branches pulled him back from his true contentment again. He would continue along his mournful walks to the old timber dock overlooking the lake-view.

He would throw stones into the water or scream until he couldn't anymore to let out his aggravation and resentment. He felt like a misplaced, dazed little boy again. He prayed for God to give him a sign – a sign that *everything will be alright.*

Chapter 10

One ordinary June day, when he decided to visit his mother's grave he told her what had been going on in his life as if she could hear him. He just sat in the grass as he swiftly laid some red tulips on his mothers tombstone with his legs crossed while laying his pocket-watch on some books he brought with him. He noticed there were birds chirping all around him; he remembered his mother told him once that would be her singing to him whenever he needed to hear a song. Then there was a soothing breeze that reassured his soul and in that second he knew everything would be okay.

He scurried home, busted open the door which frightened Amy, then he picked her up and wrapped his arms around her.

He told her, “Let’s waste no tears over the grief’s of yesterday, our unborn child is now an angel up above with God watching her, if it didn’t happen it was never meant to be, let's try to take one step forward not two steps back. We could have another child. We must always remember that when you get in a stiff place and everything appears to go against you, until it seems as though you cannot hold on a minute longer, never give up, because that's just the place and time that the tide will turn. Obstacles don't have to stop you. If you run into a wall, don't turn around and give up. Figure out how to climb it, go through it, or work

around it. Death is just a challenge. It tells us not to
waste time...It advises us to tell each other right now
that we should say how much we love each other. Amy, there is always an awe-inspiring rainbow after
every vile storm, we'll make
it through together; but now we can't let this tear us apart – I can't lose you
too. I love you, not only for
who you are, but also for who I am when I am with you; I'm the real me. Amy,

it's so easy, to think about love, to talk about love, to wish for love, but it's not always easy, to recognize love, even when we hold it in our hands and we can't let that go – in our blissful moments, we should always praise God.
In our stressful moments, we should seek God. In our painful moments, we should always trust in God. But every single moment, we should thank God for everything he has done for us."

From that day forward they lived their life by those wise words Timothy had once said.

Now Timothy was thirty-five years old and he was an amazing father to a little girl by the name of Clarissa. She was stunning just like her mother with silky brown hair, captivating cobalt eyes, fair soft skin; she was a gorgeous petite girl. Amy and Timothy were fantastic parents to Clarissa; every predicament they ran into they figured out a way to resolve it. Clarissa was taught virtues to be thankful for every blessing – she was a visionary, creative, bright, clever, rational, and delicate just like Amy. Clarissa wanted to have a love as untainted and genuine as her parents someday.

Timothy and Amy watched Clarissa grow-up

right in front of their eyes; they saw her attend the Seventh Day Adventist Church daily, graduate Rye High School, get accepted into Julie Arts, they saw her graduate, perform on Broadway, get married, and have kids of her own; Clarissa's husband is the one who now runs Timothy's charities.

Timothy was now eighty years old; he still was happily married to the love of his life, Amy.

He and Amy were walking around town;

going to a tiny old-fashioned
coffee shop
called *Shirley,* on their way
there they were looking back at their lives and remembering some of the silly things they would do
when they were younger, remembering the wild, bold
teenagers they use to be.

Amy was giggling at some of their old stories as
she gritted her wrinkly aged hands onto Timothy's
russet suede jacket sleeve,

but he sensed something was a bit off when he felt a chilly gust of wind. As they continued to stroll across the tedious gray worn out cement sidewalk Timothy started singing to her *You Light Up My Life,* she smiled so delightfully in Timothy's sparkling eyes when out of nowhere – she just let go of his sleeve, she stopped laughing, and collapsed to the ground. She was gasping for air like

a fish out of water, as
she gripped her chest,
she felt
an excruciating heart
pain;
everything seemed to be
moving in slow motion to
Timothy, he held Amy in
his arms he kept
repeating,
"Everything will be
alright,
I promise you…" While
swaying her in his arms
and relaxingly brushing
his
aged, yet fragile hands
against her powdery
white
frenzied hair.

The ambulance

wouldn't let him come with them when they arrived they said it would be best if he stayed home, he kept refusing; but they assured him she will be fine – she just had a stroke, however they made it in time and she'll be out of harm's way.

When he went home he just kept praying to God, he kept his faith and hopes up; he knew that God would make whatever choice he thought was most exceptional. When he was at home he looked at his pocket-watch for some comfort and guidance. He gripped that aged, rustic golden pocket-watch with all his might then rose from the cherry wooden chair he had in his dining room and glared out the window; he saw an almighty rainbow and instantly thought of his mother.

The next day he visited Amy in the hospital;

he moved up a cheap
green
plastic chair to sit next
her, he held her hand
and
told her he was pleased
to
see her doing well, he
began to grin, one could
see his eyes squinting a
bit
as they started to fill up
with a few tears, he
leaned
in a slightly to gently
kiss
her on the forehead, he
still noticed how she
always smelled like fresh
cherry blossoms
blooming
in the spring time, he

would told her cheesy jokes
just so he could see her smile. Then he reached into his pocket pulling out
a crumpled worn out piece
of notebook paper that read:

"My dearest Amy, you have brought one of the greatest joys to my life, no other person may ever witness or even experience, you gave me…love. It was God's fate for me to meet someone like you, to help me through the rough times in my life, to help me live out my dreams

and make a difference in this world. We have surpassed many troubles in our life. There are seven billion people on this planet, but none of them can even compare to you. They say some of the most beautiful things in life cannot be seen or even touched, but must be felt with the heart. In all honesty, I would rather have eyes that do not see, ears that hear no sound, or hands that cannot feel, than a heart that knows no love. The love you give me enlightens my soul, and enriches my heart with all that is pure. I don't want you to ever forget you were my first love, my true love, my world...I love you...

Sincerely,

Timothy Cornelius Stewart"

Amy began to sob without end; she felt so happy to hear Timothy say those comforting words to her, he was always there for her, since the day they met. Once Amy was calmed down a bit, she said,

"Oh, Timothy I loved you since the day I first met you too. Your love is

what keeps me going,
what
makes me feel alive. I
honestly don't know
what
I've done to deserve
someone as splendid as
you. The love you give
me
is like a piece of heaven,
something so
miraculously
beautiful. When I was
younger my mother
always told me, *'Find
someone that
is worth your tears,
worth
your laughter, worth your
loving-heart and someone
that loves you as much
as
you love them'* well, if she

was still here today I would
be proud to tell her, I found someone like that and it's – you. You and I will be
together forevermore and even when we're gone well
be together in spirit – I pinky promise."

Then they strung their pinkies together as Timothy swiftly laid a tender kiss on her cheek.

Chapter 11

A few weeks passed by Amy was finally allowed home again. Timothy would do sweet things for her again like when they were younger, they would take strolls around Central Park taking in the cool spring breeze air while seeing the trees move peacefully in place. He bought a large pasty hammock in which he tied it onto two oak trees and they would rest together there at times, staring up at the gigantic blue sky taking in the astounding landscape, while cuddling and thinking about their younger days, their accomplishments, and they would talk about their love for one another. This seemed to be a day-to-day basis thing for a while.

On November 23rd, it was a murky stormy night and Timothy was lying in bed with Amy they were grabbing each other's delicately aged hands securely. Amy was terrified by the brutal thunderstorm; Timothy kept trying to pacify her by playing her favorite song,

Fairytale by Enya on their
old stereo.

The flashes of bright white light piercing through the dim window shades, the loud rumbles of the lightening frightened them. It began to get icy cold inside
their home since the power
went out then Amy said she couldn't go on, but Timothy felt the same way
too – it was their time. He could still smell her cherry
blossom scent; he could

still see how gorgeous she looked with her dreamy blue eyes. Timothy gave her one last kiss upon her rose petal colored lips as he wept a bit, and then he slowly shut his eyes as he whispered *I love you.*

Timothy then had quick back flashes on his life – he remembered his excellent mother, Olivia, he remembered himself being a mere child, he reacquainted in thoughts of James, Ethan, the priest, Drew, Clarissa and her family, but most of all he pondered about...Amy. He knew they would be reunited soon; they would go to Heaven together, and he would see his mother again.

He then knew ***everything would truly be alright*** as he stepped into the light into his new life...

www.ingramcontent.com/pod-product-compliance
Ingram Content Group UK Ltd.
Pitfield, Milton Keynes, MK11 3LW, UK
UKHW021050270726
13967UKWH00012B/120

9 781105 378089